The Northway

Also by Lisa Bellamy

Nectar (chapbook)

The Northway

Lisa Bellamy

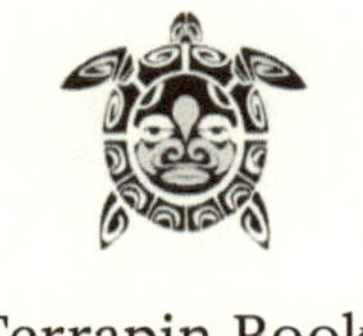

Terrapin Books

Terrapin Books
4 Midvale Avenue
West Caldwell, NJ 07006

www.terrapinbooks.com

ISBN: 978-1-947896-05-5
LCCN: 2018947680

First Edition

Cover art: *Long-Tailed Red Fox*, by John Woodhouse Audubon
c. 1848-1854, Oil on Canvas

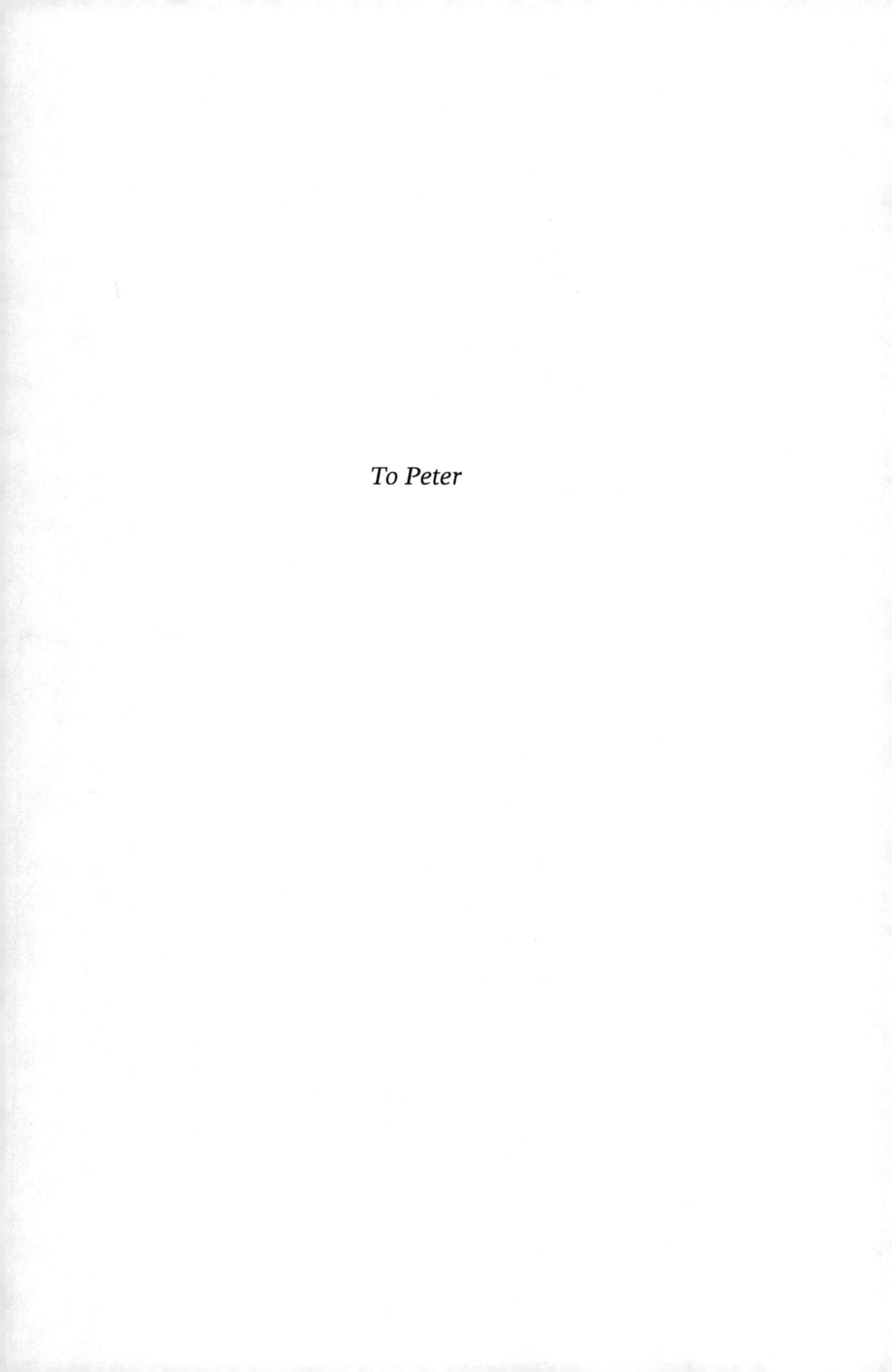

To Peter

Contents

I

Wild Pansy	7
My Sweet Little Pigeons	8
Not So Easy, Saving Sentient Beings	10
Questions for the Arborist	11
Hoot Artist	13
Obit	14
To the God of Spunk	15
Empire State	16
Our Fathers	19

II

Blueberry Crumble at the Noon-Time Diner	23
God Is an Old Pear	24
Love Song with Pigeons	25
Why I Will Not Sell the Undeveloped Parcel	26
Shamata	27
I Like the Serpent	28
Meadow Gospel	29
Eating Sadness	30
Woodchuck-a-Phobia	31
Tick	33
To My Attic	34
After	35
Spring Cleaning	36
Glory Be	37
Note to the Caretaker	38

III

Black-Eyed Susan	41
Transient Pleasures of the Animal Realm	42
Monkey Spinning a Prayer Wheel	43

The Hee-Haw 44
Bark Eater 45
Recipe 46
A Big Crow Runs Things Around Here 47
Girl Meets Bear 48
My Beloved Is Like an Otter Again 49
To the Feral Pigs of Clinton County 50
Goats 51
What I Found 53
To the Bobcat That Sprang in Front of Our Car 54
Cow Psalm 55
Who Can Forget the Grannies? 56

IV

Life as Lucy 59
All Saints Day 61
To Haplogroup K after DNA Testing 62
In the Biopsy Bardo 64
Yoho 66
To Be a Wintering Snake 67
Ezekiel 68
Land of the Peepers 69
My Holy Spirit 70
If a Black Bear Approaches 71
The Northway 73

Acknowledgments 75
About the Author 79

I stop somewhere, waiting for you.

—Walt Whitman, "Song of Myself"

Wild Pansy

As a seed, I was shot out the back end of a blue jay
when, heedless, she flew over the meadow.
She had swallowed me in my homeland when she spied me
lying easy under the sun—briefly, I called her Mother
before I passed through her gullet like a ghost.
In a blink of God's eye, I was an orphan. I trembled
where I fell, alone in the dirt. That first night
was a long night, early May and chilly, and I remember
rain filled my furrow. I called out for mercy—
only a wolverine wandered by. I cursed my luck,
I cursed the happenstance of this world, I smelled
his hot stink, but he nosed me deep into the mud—
this was the gift of obscurity. I germinated, hidden
from the giants of earth, the jostling stalks,
the various, boisterous bloomers, and this was my salvation.
After seven days and nights I pushed through—
yes. Here I am, kissable: your tiny, purple profusion.

My Sweet Little Pigeons

At the Buddhist party, I help Nyima-la,
the monk who loves Volvos as if
they were ponies, hang scarlet banners
from elms until I hear shouts:
exhausted meditators colliding
at volleyball. *They need red meat*,
says Tenzin, resident lama,
flipping his cigarette butt into the grass.
Jesus, someone says, *I thought Tibetans
were supposed to be, like, spiritual?*
Tenzin laughs, his face a brown wrinkled moon,
and I remember Byron Putnam,
my Chippewa uncle, belly swollen
with Hamm's, smoked trout and beef stew,
lying with his friends on Sheboygan's
courthouse lawn, smoking and singing,
I am ready, my sweet little pigeons,
I am ready for love; how he held me,
hands soft on my shoulders,
when I was scared, before he collapsed
from decades of drinking, dying silently
at the VA Hospital. The breeze flutters
white prayer flags, releasing 27,000 invitations
into the ghost realm. A white feral cat
crouches under the magnolias,
tracks birds overhead. May she be happy.
May the bacteria in my strawberry yogurt
be happy, cruising down my river,
digested peacefully, before
my colon's spasmodic turbulence
induces vertigo or hysteria.
May the gnats biting me take rebirth
as neonatal nurses, soothe me
the first hours of my next life—
may they be happy, free from fear.

May the elderly alligator sunbathing
on the golf course next to my mother's condo
loosen his Leviathan jaws,
allow the visiting pug
from Brooklyn to wiggle free.
May they both be happy—so may my mother,
binoculars raised, although I'm not
100% sure which one she's cheering for.
May she, too, be happy.
Tonight, Tibetans will empty
glasses and bowls to keep lonely
circling spirits from drowning.
May they be happy, free from fear.
Uncle, may you quench your unquenchable
thirst. May we shelter under
the refuge tree, free from all fear.
May I sleep, and sway in bunting,
the beloved undevoured lamb.

Not So Easy, Saving Sentient Beings

Sentient beings are numberless; I vow to save them
—Buddhist vow

When I drank, many people
tried to get me to quit.
When I drank, I drank the way
I see a frantic cardinal smash
into our living-room window:
full beak-and-body slam
against the glass, again and again.
Each time he drops, as if shot,
onto the grass, wobbles back
to his branch, flies at the window.
My bird book says he attacks
his own reflection. If I cannot
distract him with tinfoil, waves,
shouts, he might finally
meet the delusional goal
he's set: kill someone, kill
the enemy—himself, it seems.

Questions for the Arborist

Sir: do you yearn
for a trim Eden?
Do you counsel excessive
pruning and clipping,
or do you accept—
even adore—disorder?
Are you married? If so,
how would your wife
rate your passionate kisses?
Our trees struggle
for love. Would you characterize
certain species of trees
as introverts? If so,
are you gentle? Do you attempt
arboreal foreplay
before you fertilize?
Does silence make you nervous?
What role does imagination
play in your profession?
Last summer, after midnight,
the giant conifer
next to the garage
moved several feet away.
Personal altercation?
Territorial dispute?
For me, no matter—
I adopted a laissez-faire,
blasé, if you will,
attitude toward
the new arrangement.
Would you do the same?
If I told you I fear
ice jams in the river
could clog the trees' flowing chi,
would you pledge not

to repeat this, guffawing,
over beer, at the game
bird-and-gun club?
Are trees dreamers?

Hoot Artist

Tonight, through our breezy
   bedroom windows,
I hear an owl
   hoot himself silly—
a hoot artist,
   buoyant, inebriated
with hooting—
   these days,
I need to hoot like that:
   swoop the meadow,
a giddy flyover,
   tip-of-the-wing,
fibrillating the white pines—
   new maestro
of hooting trees—
   I want to rile crickets,
shiver the dry grasses,
   wake holy ghosts,
gulp sentient
   beams of the big moon,
jump-start my heart—

Obit

She died after a short illness; she died
after a long, difficult illness while
daydreaming and watching cartoons;
she died after a lingering, lovely
paralysis, a fading; she died tumbling
onto a crosswalk, where she had the
right of way; she died in her sleep;
she died in an M R I blissfully
insulated from further harassment;
she died singing *Mercy*, she died with
nary a sound; she died forgiving no
one, she died forgiving everyone; she
died, a splendid nude, dancing in
moonlight; she died at daybreak,
observed by a cat; she died speaking
in tongues—some called it mumbling.

To the God of Spunk

O, give the lady deer a rack of antlers too.
They need to get their spunk on—

they need to joust, bob and weave,
playfully practice-butt insensitive

bucks cut off from their feelings,
snorting stupid things;

honestly, given cross-eyed amateurs
taking potshots, wolverines stalking

their trembly fawns, coyotes running
in gangs nastier than Crips and Bloods,

noisy convoys rolling in after the equinox,
they need to arm themselves with more

than silence and wishful thinking.
Teach them to feint, not faint; lower their heads,

charge, perfect precision goring;
stand over hunters, licking their faces for salt.

Empire State

I am the new
frog laureate,
perched on a cushion
at the governor's
right hand,
ruby-crowned,
my winning
song so strong,
it rivals Niagara,
saving kilowatt
millions for Albany.
I sing a strong song
floating over the cities,
startling warring
gangs to a halt,
but first I need to sing
a leveling song:
People, we're broke.
We believed
in greed's effervescence,
in the worm
promising
to turn dirt
to gold—now,
we're sure we'll shiver
in damp caves
near the Canadian
border, holding
flashlights over
old Scout
manuals, batteries
low, no cash
to buy more.
We regret
our ridicule

of AM radio
pundits proclaiming
Apocalypse,
selling freeze-dried
survival rations,
recipes for
do-it-yourself
disaster Novocain—
now they seem
quite sane—
listen up, people.
I am very tired of stupid:
stupid in the streets,
stupid sea to sea—
we're lucky
Jesus hasn't yet
returned to slap us
all upside the head.
It's time to steal
blunderbusses
from museums,
blast stupid
into the sky
with our explosive
wisdom, time
to borrow the three-star
belt of Orion,
leave hesitation as collateral,
time to proclaim
Ah-Ah-Ah,
mantra of fearlessness,
time to whistle
for the wind ponies,
time to ride
to the hidden valley
and lie for a year
and a day in grass,
in wind, rain,

and snow,
then rise, singing
the old order of things
has passed away,
as old John of Patmos
sang, shivering
naked on his rock
in sea breeze,
flipping the bird
at Rome.

Our Fathers

Our fathers never spoke to us of their wars.
Each morning, they girded their loins with tool belt
and slide rule, according to their appointed trades.
In the summer, as they backed out
our driveways, we ran after them. In the winter,
they left, whistling, as we slept.
They created Japanese-style goldfish ponds,
built backyard gazebos, sang barbershop harmony,
strummed mandolins, ukuleles, but
refused to call themselves makers of beauty.
They woke us at midnight to see the Aurora Borealis,
carried us out to rose and white light waves streaming,
named for the goddess of dawn who brings life,
and the god of the north wind who brings death.
Our fathers grew restless. They started to pace,
walked outside to gawk at the stars.
When we asked, *Can we come*, they said, *No.*
When we asked why, they said, *Hush.*
Our fathers stopped kissing our mothers.
They came home midday: fired, laid-off, warned
for swearing at the foreman, said they were sick
unto death. They slammed screen doors, bedroom doors,
shed doors. They started to drink. They stood up
from couches, pushed dogs that nosed them, stumbled
outside, yodeling. Said they felt bigger
than the sky. They drank in bomb shelters, garages,
at the Legion Post, watching TV. They drank
driving us to Scouts, bottles between their knees.
They drank when we begged them not to and when
we tried to ignore them. Sometimes
they slammed us against walls, sometimes they
said they were sorry. One by one, they left:
in sedans, vans, the pick-up, walking to the bus stop.
They left in the morning as we sat, silent,

at the kitchen table, eating cereal before school.
We watched them leave with their suitcases.
They left a goodbye note for us to find
after track practice. They left at night after fights.
Some stayed, but stopped talking, or faded
fast, eyes rolled back, clutching their heart.
Others left over time, from their wasting diseases.
They said they would never forget us.
Our fathers said they loved us, and we believed them.

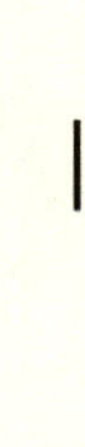

Blueberry Crumble at the Noon-Time Diner

A dearth of potatoes drove my ancestor Dennis McCarthy
onto a boat to America—
I lift my forkful of greasy hash browns in tribute:
Thank you, Dennis, for saving me from hunger, pig-tending,
cheap lace, and the Irish horror of happiness,
as my beloved and I devour eggs at the Noon-time Diner
before hiking Rooster Comb Mountain.
Across the aisle, citizens in shorts, lime-green and yellow,
buttocks splayed splendidly on red vinyl cushions—
a cook lofting a pie through swinging kitchen doors,
slapping it on the counter announcing,
Blueberry crumble, if anyone cares, then scurrying away.
Dang—that's exactly what I sometimes do!
Why not display the pie?
Jesus, our wonder-working yidam, was clear on this point:
Don't hide your crumble under a bushel.
His enemies called him a glutton, but I've read that can mean,
a person with a remarkably great capacity for something.
My mother wanted me to emulate Audrey Hepburn
(tasteful, tiny, a touch of anorexia), but I wanted
to be Sophia Loren, crimson silks, a flash of panties,
wet breasts brimming, swimming to shore in sunlight—
oh, I'm smelling the sugar now, Baby—syrupy berries
plucked from bushes nestled on Baxter Mountain,
cake drizzled with caramel at the Saranac Lake revival,
trout spattering in honey and butter at my grandparents' house,
Dennis's silver communion watch displayed on a shelf,
sugar, mammary sugar, starfish stream from the nipple.
I smell Dennis's whiskey breath as he makes love to his wife,
I lick salt dripping from my beloved's neck; I have capacity,
I definitely have capacity. I smell gunpowder from muskets
blazing from Fort William Henry, bear grease in the hair
of Mohawk men camped near Lake Champlain—
why not? I am Paul Bunyan's little sister,
swinging my axe at the root of delusion;
Dennis, Dennis hello, I am your rude American daughter.

God Is an Old Pear

At midnight, I wander barefoot
  into the cold kitchen.
My beloved sleeps, but I
  stop myself from waking him.
I know I will not rest tonight—
  I have been awful. Dawn
to dusk, I had a stone in me,
  instead of heart and lungs.
Opening the fridge, I see
  a greenish-brown pear.
Cupping it in my hand,
  curious if it is still
soft, I kiss its mottled skin.

Love Song with Pigeons

I hear cooing and scuffling, as I pause on my building's steps—
at first, with the fluttering, I hope for angels, a visitation,
but realize I am listening to pigeons, crammed in a window box,
mating over my head. I'm glad I don't have to have sex
in a window box. I am sure Peter is, too—glad, that is.
Peter's my husband and we have fun sex in a bed,
under the off-white comforter with blue-green floral trim.
We are lucky, we are blessed; we are happily married—
both of us for the second time—although last night in the car
he mentioned singing, *The King of Love My Shepherd Is*
at the wedding. I snapped, *Jesus damn it to hell, that was
your first wedding.* Pouting and so forth. Peter bit his lip—
Oh, I'm so sorry baby—as he drove to West 53rd Street.
I stared out the window; people looked blurry and stupid.
I thought how nice, to live alone in a little Hell's Kitchen studio.
But then I remembered his first love letter, quoting Hart Crane,
came with a box of JuJubes (my favorite) taped to the side.
I forgave him—I'd once called him Sam, my first husband's name.
We reached the diner at West 53rd and Peter parked like a duke;
no one parallel parks like my husband and we smooched—
sadness over—as a spaniel, undocked plumy tail aloft, strutted by.

Why I Will Not Sell the Undeveloped Parcel

I promised the skunks a place to stink.

I promised certain fur-bearing citizens,
i.e., the possum consortium,
easements in perpetuity through weedy
boulevards to the creek.

I committed to long-term housing for the
skeptics, the chattering class of the
underbrush (skittish field mice,
recalcitrant porcupines, sharp-tongued
pheasant hens).

I promised wild turkeys a private event
space for meetings in bushes—they
have crucial business to discuss,
clucking and fussing, lofting feathers.

To the proud, newly antlered deer,
I promised a dojo to train in four
dignities: contentment, joy, wisdom
and outrageousness.

I promised myself my own Camp
Lollygag, for me to tramp, trip
on knotted weeds, sink in slick
to my ankles, practice bewilderment,
embargo goal setting—

what needs to rot, I say, can rot.
I promised the moon a pack of
enamored, serenading coyotes.
I promised the sun a slice of insouciant
soil on which to shine.

Shamata

On our twenty acres, I will tend an unruly pony herd.
They will buck and bite, but I will not back away. I will brush
their rough coats, comb their stiff manes—they will snap
when I bring hay. I will note their foolishness and train them—
light, skillful flicks of the whip—to pull me to town
and back, to Essex, to wherever I choose to go,
in a wooden cart painted yellow. We will rattle under
sun, clouds, and rain and I will bounce behind
their industrious flanks, name the sturdiest, *Pilgrim*.
Later, I will pour mash into their buckets, pluck burrs
from hooves, bandage leg wounds. They will begin to gaze
shyly at me in the barn. After seven years, I will blow
into their trembling ears to release them, but they will decide
to remain: guardians of the perimeter. At dawn,
I will teach them their prayers, at noon, shoo black flies
from their eyes before they leave to traverse our pastures
and fields, nibble clover from the lonely meadow long ago
married to the faithless wind who now rarely comes home.
Foxes will watch from the forest. At dusk, smoking
a corncob pipe like my grandmother smoked in Alberta,
I will wait on the porch with my beloved for the ponies' news
and reports from the realm. At night, I will sing to them
of pony kings before they sleep.

I Like the Serpent

He is my pretty,
green little thing—
when I doze in the meadow,
he perceives, he stirs
in his hole, he slides,
sticking his tongue
in my ear—I startle awake;
I tickle his vestigial chin
with vernal stalks,
he rises, rippling—
You, he hisses,
I whisper, *Here I am.*

Meadow Gospel

Kick off your shoes—call me tickler
   of bare feet; call me listener
to secrets you whisper to sunflowers,
   call me amphitheater for discordant crickets'
late afternoon concerts.
   You, too, could sing from the shadows—
you've forgotten you're not the only soul
   to lug a little sack of trouble.
This is my body, and yours:
   dame's rocket, sweet grass and sage;
this is my blood, and yours:
   the dream-inducing milk of dandelions.
Lie in me, in remembrance of yourself—
   you know you've forgotten
everything you knew before you were born.

Eating Sadness

I select only fresh, locally-sourced sadness—
nothing tinned or flown in. Grilled mournfulness,

marinated in a sauce of light self-scrutiny,
garnished with butter-rosettes of regret,

brushed with hindsight? Delicious.
However, at times, only pan-seared drama will do.

Vinegary crust cut with spite and bitter herbs,
hiding a surprisingly moist filling,

presents a caper-studded, surprising regret.
I do find that without a mélange, a little caraway,

a little rue, a little paprika laced with chagrin,
moping is bland. And stylish presentation is crucial—

behold my sleek Sadness Julienne—
who wouldn't admire sassy strips of dancing sadness?

Woodchuck-a-Phobia

An afflicted state. Condition
in which the eerie whistle of the creature—
New England farmers called it "Whistle Pig,"
suspected it of congress with the Devil—
or the sight of it sunning itself,
or the glimpse of its wet snout
or lumpish torso waddling
into the brush, or the insult
of yet another filthy hole
dug steps away from the house,
causes extreme fear of the woodchuck,

i.e., jitters. Dizziness. Inability to concentrate
after an encounter, even if
one is "safely" inside the house.
Agitation thrumming like a relentless
sewing machine. The memory of its stink.
Restless dreams of a muddy paw
over one's mouth. Worry
that the woodchuck will tunnel so extensively
under the house, will construct
such a complex, branching multi-layered
tunnel, that the house will collapse
due to foundation failure.

Collapse is the chaos and danger—
often mortal—one experiences
when foundations, cement basement pillars,
door frames, light fixtures, ceilings,
window sills and roofs lose sturdy reliability.
Not only structural elements
start to wobble: promises,
affirmations, vows, and articles of faith
also lose sturdy reliability.
Once-content couples irritate each other

beyond the usual irritations.
Fissures and cracks appear
in previously truthful representations.
Betrayals eventually occur.

Sturdy reliability is the characteristic
of trustworthy things. It promotes trust
in representations and assumptions.
A ceiling represents that the room
under the ceiling will continue
to exist as a room, not rubble
under which one moans weakly—
if one can moan at all. Sturdy reliability is
an assumption that the ceiling will
act in accordance with its Nature.

Nature is the essence of things.

In accordance with the principles of Nature,
one admits that, in addition to eating,
defecation, sex, sleep,
labor, and pleasure, the woodchuck's
essence is to make tunnels.

Tick

Like an addict, famished—
from the under-
petal of a flower,
it stretches trembling
front legs, waves,
invites, interrogates
teeming air
without discrimination—
faint, dizzy,
jonesing for blood—
a desperate stance
mimicking
the true joy of seduction.

To My Attic

In your dreamy emptiness—
a sketch of a room,
unfinished business,
rough pine beams,
plastic taped over the windows,
spiders spinning
in the eaves; in the corners,
mouse scat like cairns
marking trails to
encampments behind the walls—
I would be your lone sailor,
cruising your circumference;
I would be your anchorite,
silent, as I've always wanted,
like Dame Julian,
who perceived God's splendor
in an acorn on the floor
when, alone in her cottage,
she finally
gave herself nothing else to look at—

After

After she noted the basement door closed yet again—
   after her stomach twisted, her neck tingled,
after she opened the door; after he jumped
   from his chair, slammed the computer top; after she shouted,
Show me what you are doing, after he shook his head,
   after she placed her hands on his neck and squeezed,
and his face grew pink, but his tongue did not protrude;
   after he broke her hold and ran up the stairs;
after she growled, *Halt*, and noted her grave,
   even martial, imperative—after he reached the mudroom,
after she shouted, fists clenched, after she hated,
   noticed the frost-spiked back door, the black, starry night
beyond, and with pleasure recalled a movie in which
   a helmet-less astronaut is sucked, howling, into the void;
after she noted his bare feet and found this satisfying,
   the image of his bare feet in snow, and she pushed him to
the door and sub-zero air; after he, deploying
   defensive maneuvers, braced his back against the wall
and she started to slap him—inexpertly, given that her previous
   combat experience had primarily been with her sister—
he said, *OK*. They adjourned to the living room,
   where he started to talk.

Spring Cleaning

I fling every invasive house mite into her web.
The spider spins, she waits for me,
she knows I bring her the disappointments,
the skittering, multi-legged resentments,
half-eaten, rotten leavings.
She engorges herself with the negativities,
eats the little deaths for me—
an agreement I negotiated with her ancestors.

Glory Be

Glory be to the squishy road, the sunken-feet road,
the mud road—meandering, curvy and buxom—
along this greenish, trout-happy river.
Glory be to the river road on which I stroll—
when I stop to watch flowing water bubble up,
flirt with a half-submerged log,
my blood pressure thanks me.
Make way, I say, *for the not-straight,
the not-narrow*, i.e., me—call me *slowpoke,
poky candy*, call me *creamy caramel,
on a stick*—let the moist air lick me,
let my head buzz like a hot hive.
Let me, for these few minutes,
not discern the difference between thoughts and mosquitos.

Note to the Caretaker

Tonight, we drive back to the city—in our absence,
please negotiate a final settlement with the mole: we
concede all territory from the driveway to the garage,
and trust this meets with his satisfaction. We have acted
in good faith. We coped with his repeated tunneling
despite the injunction; we coped with his refusal to
schedule daytime meetings; we rose at midnight with
flashlights for conferences while he hid behind a bush
and spoke through intermediaries. I understand he must
live and work in isolation, and I know he cannot cease
his digging, for his claws are godly spades and dirt his
pleasing material and he knows his dirt contains
nutrients, i.e., organic matter, for his art: shredded
entrails, scraps of fur on bone, broken teeth, tears and
spit. He knows his dirt remains malleable and no one
should confuse it with filth. In dirt, he can freely breathe
and re-oxygenate his air. In dirt, the Holy Spirit blows
through him. Behind him as he digs, he creates mounds,
and many are the mounds built for the glory of his God.
He is grateful for the velvety fur in which he slides
through his tunnel, and his objection to fracking is 100%
pragmatic, for he is an earthworks artist in the style and
tradition of his clan, vain only in the matter of his tail.
He will twist his neck backward to admire it. He is
furious in his concentration, for his craft, he knows, is
essential for the Earth to circle the Sun, and when he
works, day and night, in one-pointed Samadhi, he neither
eats nor sleeps.

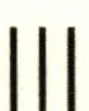

Black-Eyed Susan

I just cannot bloom endlessly, you know—
this is November, I'm pale, a dry stalk—
I can barely stand, I'm shaking, I need Me time,
I need to center myself—this summer was horrific:
it was all about the aphids, crawling,
depositing God knows what without permission,
from who knows what hollows of slime;
it was all about the jays—"by mistake"
they smashed into me, to grab the crickets—
I had to hear the swallowing, see the bulging gullets.
This summer was all about the bees, their selfishness,
overall lack of tenderness. Oh, bees are sly.
They say they buzz for beauty, for splendor;
they preen, like frilly-hatted debutantes—a racket,
people, a con job—they trampled on my privates,
scurried back and forth, mobsters with booty
(my pollen!), to their dank clubs, their little "hives."
This summer was all about the deer, the nibbling,
the slobbering, ticks crawling in and out of their noses—
sweet Jesus, a sight no one should have to endure—
and who, in the meadow, thought to kiss my petals?
People, I'm on my own here. I need T-L-C.
Look, dormant does not mean down for the count.
I will re-seed myself, re-invent myself—hardiest
of the hardy perennials—but I need to be pumped
from below, long and slow, with cool water brimming
under the meadow. I need the slathering,
mudpack sliding in my flowerets,
wet leaves—dammit, someone needs to soothe my pistil.

Transient Pleasures of the Animal Realm

If I were one
of the stiff-legged robins
I see marching
across our meadow,
I would be
their crimson queen,
my feathers fluffed
and pomaded—a fencer,
given my extraordinary
beak—and if the woman
that sexted my husband
were a creeping thing
on the ground, a tiny
stick of crawling meat,
I would open my dark
maw to skewer,
then devour her—
within seven minutes,
she would be shat,
explosively, into
the jonquil. Watching
me prance through Joe-Pye,
aphids clinging to leaves—
my tender scribes—
would record the jubilee.

Monkey Spinning a Prayer Wheel

I stumble out of the theater after *Waiting for Godot.*
Jeez, I gripe to Peter, *That's it? We're all just wind and gristle?*
After a minute he says, *Yep,* and I know he's trying to remember
whether he'd stuck the parking ticket in his wallet
or pocket. He gallantly takes the notion of a meaningless
universe in stride, while I feel like a
bewildered monkey spinning a prayer wheel,
trying to contemplate so-called larger questions.
At the Tibetan Buddhist center downtown, we recite
the Heart Sutra: *Perceiving that personality is inherently*
empty saves beings from suffering, as monks, red cheeks puffed
like twenty Dizzy Gillespies, accompany us,
blowing horns, strident heralds announcing ego's apocalypse,
and I'm thinking, *What?* What are we *talking* about here?
I recite daily my version of Marvin Gaye's mantra
as fast as I can: *what's going on, what's going on, what's*
really going on? Oh God, send me someone wise and
shimmering, the archangel carrying the sword
to cut through confusion; or, if no archangel handy,
send me a soothing, jazzy brunch contralto, an arm to pull
me onto the raft as I thrash in *dukkha's* river,
my memory of chipping a tooth on our backyard granite
rock, wailing, as my mother runs from sunbathing,
reading Leon Uris, her freckled arms,
the smell of suntan oil—where is she? Where is she?

The Hee-Haw

Run before dawn
to the wet meadow,
summon the donkeys,
still snoring
in their little shed;
whistle to wake
dreaming Jenny,
dreaming Jack—
wait to hear
the hee-haw,
the bray, the blast
cutting through
discursive prattle,
nothing but reruns—
go ahead, live
inside the hee-haw,
slide through
the warm day,
like sugar on Jenny's
or Jack's tongue;
dance a new jig,
bare toes tingling,
high-five
the streaming air,
let the wind
lift your nightie,
sly gift
of inspiration.

Bark Eater

Yes, a snooty Mohawk word for bumpkin,
for yokel lacking the smarts and gumption to hunt—

but I say, *A bark eater makes do.*

Consider this: a hungry traveler on a hard journey
who, as the pale winter sun goes down,

sees only trees and snow but does not lose her cool;
she refuses to starve. Without hesitation,

she sharpens the knife, slices a white pine and roasts
the bark, like a banquet of bear steak.

This barren meal is hardly a tale told by an idiot—she is
pleased to call it Feast.

Girl, my mother used to say, *you always land on your feet.*
The bark eater toasts the Dog Star and asks for protection,

thus surviving yet another frozen night without tears.
She knows she can cry all she wants in the spring.

Missy, my father used to say, *play the cards you're dealt.*

A bark eater spies the Morning Star and spits into the wind—
her prayer of water and air. She doesn't need a compass,

she knows she's walking north—she's traveling light.

Recipe

Mix impatience with forced pleasantries
(observation of twittering birds,
bright, sunny sky, and so forth),
with heart palpitations, trembling hands,
revenge fantasies, obsessive thinking.
Add fight-or-flight, add shortness of breath,
add the startle reflex. You startle now,
everywhere, at everything. Add fist-clenching,
cupboard-slamming, foot-stomping.
Ask, *Where?* Ask, *Why?*
Ask, *Where's the infernal, suffering sugar?*

A Big Crow Runs Things Around Here

A big crow runs things around here:
his crew supervises from their coniferous
perches. They communicate all day
regarding our comings and goings—
they exhibit especially stringent surveillance
of our neighbor Bernice Frechette,
the giantess, when she ambles over—
and this morning, I watched three or four
crows fly in to receive their assignment
from the Big Guy, who fluttered down
from his birch, branch by branch—showy
but effective. I saw blinding purple shine
through his feathers, a few black tufts
rose on his head: he was a Legionnaire,
loud, uttering sharp, imperative cries.
I tried to translate from my camp chair.
I would not mind his instruction—
I need a reprieve. I am too distraught,
these days, to decide anything.
How lovely, to be told what to do—
Hop to it, baby, he would say,
and gladly would I hop,
screeching,
clearing trespassing chickadees.

Girl Meets Bear

Me, just 18,
up past midnight,
dancing, singing—
my parents gone
for the weekend—
and he, all brown
fur and big snout,
staring at me
through the screen door.
I went for bad boys,
but this was a stretch;
nevertheless,
next morning, an overturned
can in the driveway
told just part
of the story. He came
for garbage,
but stayed for love.

My Beloved Is Like an Otter Again

The otter believes in god, the river almighty,
eternal and streaming, a god
who judges neither the quick nor the dead nor almost-dead—

he adores shoals sheltering impromptu amusement parks,
hidden tunnels of love
in the mud burrows, shady meditation spots on the shore—

he trusts the potluck abundance of take-out:
crawfish, grubs, wisps of midges,
even a murdered mole on the bank, its guts emptying into soil—

with equanimity, he withstands swarms of no-see-ums,
dives and splashes,
evades, turns their harassment into yet another game—

my beloved is like an otter again,
mind and body no longer clouded; sleek and light,
he moves through space as if it were milk.

To the Feral Pigs of Clinton County

Root on, ladies and gentlemen—yes, to sex with multiple partners;
    yes, to nipples the color and size of Cuban cigars;
yes, to fields overrun with your sucklings—when I say, *feral pig*,
    I see darting eyes, envision a remorseless nature, but if I say,
wild boar, I hear golden flugelhorns. Where is it written
    you were meant to be constrained? Yes, to grunts and drooling;
yes, to dripping snouts shoveling beetles out of loam;
    yes, to nocturnal plunder of apple and pear orchards,
gorging on Anjou, Empire, and Crispin—is this not your right,
    are you not descended from imported Burgundian boars?
Did they not bust loose? Every aristocrat is a secret anarchist:
    yes, to pissing long and yellow on domestic and civic order;
yes, to butting-over of stone walls mortared by heroes of the Republic;
    yes, to your ancestors' refusal to eat bucketed swill flung
at them in their pens—root on, ladies and gentlemen, root on—

Goats

Last night, Daisy had a doeling,
Dixie had two bucklings,
the local artisanal goat farm website
notes this early morning.
Each day, I check new kidding dates,
for the farm's laboring mothers.
If I had the acreage and leisure, I would
be a goat-herder: I admire
their perseverance, willingness to forego
conventional pleasantries in pursuit
of their goals. Goats care nothing for
your good opinion—in their search
for achievable outcomes, goats interrogate
a backpack, purse, trouser pocket
to the point of rudeness, prizing nosiness,
creative entrepreneurship,
stick-to-it-ness, refusing ordinary
focus on time & materials, project management.
I revel in their lyric nature: amorous
goats soft-shoeing, hoofing it,
flank-to-sturdy-flank across meadows;
lady goats great with child,
pawing the ground, lifting their tails,
nuzzling their big stomachs into hay,
groaning, panting, licking slick newborns.
Thunderstorms bring intense pleasure—
only the ancient god of electricity
could truly train a goat:
standing on his noisy chariot, pulled
by two horned, nose-flaring
warriors, he careened across the sky,
up-ending cultivated fields,
orchards and flimsiness—to this day
goats love to see things of this world
strewn before them, as if

flung only to satisfy their curiosity.
Still ladies-in-waiting to labor:
Marjoram, Cascade, Carter, Voyageur,
Pinnacle, Fern, Pink
and Deedie—all eager to exhale,
hoof lightly back to the fields,
to frolicking in summer, milk-sucking,
grass-eating, bleating, back-rubbing,
leaping for sparks that we, in our ignorance,
call stars, to swallow them whole—
they will never stop until
they light the world from their bellies.

What I Found

In your drawer of overlooked things,
I found a story you never read,
because you didn't have time.
I found the ripe tomatoes
Papa picked in August,
when he looked shyly at you,
as you bit into the first one.
I found the red-ribboned red dress,
the one you did not buy for me,
the Christmas I turned six.
Look how beautiful I am in it now.
See how beautiful I am.

To the Bobcat That Sprang in Front of Our Car

Peter's right leg slams the brake—
we skid toward the ditch,
and here you are, staring at us in the dark,

yellow eyes like O-Bon lanterns for the dead.
I like to think that you,
tawny and stylish, a spotted bristle,

had been racing an owl, as if to prove
that fur and muscle,
a good ground game, trump a pair of wings

and spooky voice. I admire your alert appraisal.
I want what you have;
that's something they say in AA.

Had I seen the bird I'd write about it instead;
but you are the one
who jumped in front of the car—I want

your steady gaze. I will see nothing in this world
if I refuse stillness,
refuse to look directly at what is before me.

You don't look like a cat that needs to drink gin.
Peter cuts the headlights
and now, most likely, you tire of us.

Like a host who coughs politely,
looks at the clock,
you discreetly swivel your tufted head to the sky,

spring back into darkness,
like Zen master Hakuin who entered this world,
then left it, without a trace.

Cow Psalm

To the sly rebels, hoof-stompers, tail-switchers
quick-slapping the faces of farmers;
to the nippers, biters, udder-clenchers,

haters of forced bovine production;
to the saboteurs pinning their milkmen
with slow, inexorable two-step waltzes to

barn walls; to the kickers who overturn
brimming buckets, then stare,
with limpid, big-eyed pretend surprise—

I say, *Amen*, for they spurn enticements and treats:
watermelon, ground corn; they sneer at
jangling ornaments, flower crowns, cowbells;

they disdain daisy chains placed on their necks;
they refuse ear-scratching, stroking,
petting. Remembering their stolen sons,

they are historians of loss, they refuse to forgive.
Summer grasses are bitter weeds to them;
night and day, they worship their golden calves,

they despise their useless milk—every exhalation is *No*.
For the insurrectionists of the creamery,
their strong, unstoppable hearts, I say, *Hallelujah*.

Who Can Forget the Grannies?

I shudder when I think of the eight-foot beavers
grunting, squatting, splashing, spitting in our river—
tiny-brained, squinting Pleistocene thugs—
baring incisors longer than a human arm,
they infested ponds and rivers, smothered
gasping fish with their acid-spiked, toxic urine;
they slapped their murderous tails—bleating,
they dragged themselves up the riverbank,
smelling sweet grass; they charged crawling babies,
the tiny baby bones, trampling, they didn't care—
hurray for naked, yelling Stone Age grannies—
they dropped hammer stones, grabbed sharpened sticks.
Who can forget their skinny, bouncing breasts?
They beat the giant beavers, they speared, they smeared
thick beaver blood over each other's faces, over
bony, serviceable buttocks—who can forget the grannies?

IV

Life as Lucy

Bernice, my neighbor, misheard my name when we met:
Lucy? she asked, as I introduced myself.
My ears perked up like an eager dog off the leash
hearing the Beloved Friend call her name,
suddenly alert amidst the city's distraction and babble,
fragrant pigeons just out of reach, sirens,
couples growling face to face in the street.
There's nothing soft or vague about *Lucy*.
Lucy's a dachshund digging
under the rosebush Grandma planted,
salivating for tasty mole scraps, ignoring cries
and folded newspaper swatting behind her.
Lucy's a bookie, sporting a porkpie hat,
cigar clamped in her mouth.
She's running on spit, playing the odds,
for more time to make good on her bets.
Lucy is—bucky.
You're getting bucky again, my mother would say.
Brown silky hair chopped at the ears,
bangs cut razor-straight,
jaw set, lower lip ready for battle,
at seven, in a fringed cowgirl suit,
cap pistols ready to draw from my holster.
She meant stubborn, dug-in,
as in, *No, I won't eat the creamed corn*,
like my childhood guru, Peter Rabbit,
canny model of spiritual development,
who, refusing a life of deprivation
(pathetic nose pressed to the fence),
smashed constraints of class and birth,
feasted without regret on all the French beans,
lettuce, and radishes he could eat.
Lucy, meaning light, or radiance,
bright with righteous rage for newborns,
who, eyes opening in wonder,
flinch in pain and confusion

as nurses drop silver nitrate into their eyes.
Yes, I am anointed, but no,
I will not stop to shovel manure.
I follow one who parties with thieves
and tax collectors, drunkards carrying torches
into the bridal chamber.
Those with eyes to see, let them see.
Yes, I will pick up the slack, but no,
I will not wait for the kingdom.
No, I will not save the best for the last.
I am the first *and* the last.
I am burning, a 10,000-year filament.
At daybreak, I shook hands with Ezekiel—
he said, *Girl, you're doing just fine.*

All Saints Day

Just before dawn, they walk across a spooky field.
They jostle among us until sundown,
listen to our chatter, nudge each other, read the news
over our shoulders; they window shop,
zoom through revolving doors, sniff new perfumes,
slip into swanky dresses. At noon on Third Avenue,
walking to Hale and Hearty, I smell my mother's
cigarette smoke. *Hey. You. Not so fast*, I say,
Did you love me? Did I ever walk into a room—
and I was the one person you wanted to see?
The old question. A great cloud of witnesses holds its breath
for her answer—and, as if she were a hurricane,
and I a tree, she blows through me:
a wordless storm of regret.

To Haplogroup K after DNA Testing

Greetings, my snappish, results-oriented sisters—
we wander through crowds
unknown to each other,
slurping fruit pastries in Salzburg,
shopping for bridal gowns at Kleinfelds,
hobbling down Terre Haute hospital halls,
intravenous cocktail cords dangling,
slamming phones,
trading oil futures from Calgary skyscrapers,
our matrilineal DNA still reeling,
30,000 years after that trek from the steppes.
We feel exhausted and irritable
as those women surely were,
their heads covered against biting wind
as they led oxen,
tended sick and dying children,
counseled men lost
with only stars and clouds to guide them,
cooked road-trip broth of grass and tough goat,
and all of that without coffee.
Could we regroup, reconvene now,
for a reunion of sorts?
Could I send you joke emails,
news clippings, coupons,
a file of *Joy of Cooking* recipes to avoid?
My own close cohort is thinning,
Mother lunging for the last bargain at Gimbels,
aunt duck hunting at dawn in Wisconsin,
German grandmother, furious, scraping her bundt pan,
three women, cigarette smoke swirling,
gossiping, drinking coffee—Lutherans!
Obsessive, pork-eating, streusel-baking Lutherans—
all gone. With sisters and cousins flung,
like dazed starlings, across North America,
some numbed by vodka and Percocet,

and others, sweet knuckleheads,
waiting for Jesus in Butte or Kenosha,
I shoot my flares into the night sky,
hoping you—any of you,
my dear Haplogroup K, will find me.

In the Biopsy Bardo

I leave Dr. T's office sporting a bandaged breast—
step into sunlight and yellow forsythia,
seeing vividly into strollers, babies smiling,

nannies, mothers, babies spitting and wailing.
Perhaps sooner than I imagined,
I will find myself plunked in a wheelie myself,

drooling and pooping; in the bardo,
say Tibetans, your idea of yourself as your former body
fades, as your future body takes shape.

My mole, my little brown house on the prairie,
once round and cozy, is now asymmetrical,
officially scary, sliced neatly and shipped

to Mount Sinai Pathology. *None can save you now,
Missy,* Captain Hook shouts to Wendy,
as I plan my funeral hymns, i.e.,

"Rock My Soul in the Bosom of Abraham,"
stand-out selection of our fifth grade's
American Hymns and Spirituals Unit,

where *bosom* collapsed boys over their desks,
nervous and giggling, hands over eyes.
My bosom stings and smarts,

ten days for lab results and, given my analysis
of Dr. Seuss's oeuvre, in which waywards bowed
to the tap-dancing god of mayhem,

I'm not surprised the Israelites abandoned themselves
so quickly to worship of a golden mammal,
when Moses failed to return promptly from the mountain.

Poor Moses, it was surely a wrench to find Bastet,
lion-queen of cats, sashaying through camp,
yowling for sexual congress with her consort,

lapping goat milk, bell tinkling around her neck,
bell of wakefulness, delight in the moment.
Subsequent exegesis got it wrong.

Think *golden cat*, not *calf*—if there's a god,
I think it might be an unpredictable cat,
unneutered, licking his paws; spraying at will.

Yoho

Deep lake, dark cloud:
Grant us your stillness.
May we walk, unharmed,
through fields favored
by bears. May lightning
pass over us, may we never
be hungry, may we eat
as we ate supper
at the railway diner
near Kicking Horse Pass:
potato-leek soup,
fried bean burgers,
two cups of coffee,
under a flickering bulb;
for the sweet bye-and-bye,
let there be light.

To Be a Wintering Snake

To leave a note; to shut the door behind me—
to quit the fray; to abstain, temporarily,
from the fraught ways and means of this world;
to be a wintering snake
who slithers easily through dry stalks,
crawls to a hidden cave,
snuggling into a perfect crevice,
hidden, in twigs and leaves, for a season.

Ezekiel

I will send the rain of authority,
rain to chase the devil back to hell—
smeary goose-shit rain,
rain of snarling martens,
rain of mud and tar,
rumors-of-war rain,
rain to trigger his disgust,
the rain of defiant lovers,
naked tongue rain,
his worst-nightmare rain—
I will send the rain of warrior-babies
(tiny swords,
tin breastplates of righteousness).
I will send flummoxing rain,
rain to ding his minions,
spiritual warfare rain—
I will send rain in-it-for-the-long-haul,
rain biding its time,
watchful crow rain,
rain beyond his paygrade,
deceptively soft,
Mata Hari rain—
I will send slain-in-the-spirit rain,
Holy Ghost rain,
prophecy rain,
om-shanti-shanti-rain,
no-tweeting rain,
turn-off-the-TV rain,
rain to scour the demon-stink,
rain of purification,
everlasting white birch rain,
god help me,
help me, rain—
I will send blasting rain—
scram, I will say,
beat it, I will say—*be gone.*

Land of the Peepers

Sweetie, after supper,
after dark, after
animal hearts beat hard,
let's shimmy; let's twirl out
the back door to the damp field;
let's stroll, arm in arm,
to our red, willy-nilly flashy cruiser;
let's drive to the fecund bogs—
take me to the frogs,
to the land of the peepers—
high soprano saxophone
sex blasts, blown
from such tiny bellies;
Sweetie, stroll
with me
to the swamp—
let's bellow—

My Holy Spirit

At dawn, *my* holy spirit smokes tiny cigars,
exhales into the clouds—
a gust that jump-starts sleeping beasts,
fires up the chlorophyll,
froths and churns the oceans' brine.
She proceeds from a blind date,
polyandrous, in the Pleistocene,
among warm, nutrient-laden rain drops,
sentient dolphins, mineral-rich
dust streaming from explosive supernovas.
These days, she drives her own car,
registered with the Department of Insouciance;
she speaks through the peepers.
My holy spirit loves naked—
who's her Daddy? Nobody knows.

If a Black Bear Approaches

*When meeting a bear, one should "speak in normal tones so you
sound human. What you say doesn't matter, just speak."*
—Adirondack Explorer

O Gigantic—filthy,
slightly-slobbering,
big-tongued Teddy
sniffing the air—
I hear luscious bee hives
cluster twenty miles yonder,
east, over Clement Mountain—
why not, Sir, point
your nose to the honey,
why not ponder this *koan*
as you journey: why *did*
the bear go over the mountain?
What *did* he hope
to find? What generous spirit
whispered, *wanderlust*?
Why not pursue
the "big story,"
scratch your back
against the hard questions?
O, impressive Baloo,
through your heart
pumps the blood
of ancient giants,
who once loved
children of men—
see me, not as
your snack,
but your Beatrice,
lamplighter for
your quest. Why not
aspire to roll
in the thing-in-itself,
the *ding an sich*,

as if in clover?
Go, go now,
go, go, go,
my splendid, plus-size
Paddington; turn
your head to the sky;
go forth—eastward
ho, to the honey.

The Northway

If I drive with my eyes closed,
I imagine the road better:
I hear music, an *Oh-Ah-Hum*,
subliminal vibrating GPS
of the strawberry moon—
my sonic bat waves guide me,
while my beloved passenger dozes,
and I soar through midnight shadows,
purple breezes, languid
rafts of loons, and past
the firefly-lit town of Minerva,
where locals insist angels
flourish fiery swords,
signaling signs and wonders,
marking the boundary between
previous humdrum exits,
and the extraordinary one ahead,
and I sing, *you're a shining star*
no matter who you are,
to disconsolate Holsteins
slumped against fences,
and I soar: light from light,
true gal from true gal,
as foxes crouched in bushes
yip encouragement—
till I slip through a shimmering door,
clouds of white crickets,
thistles whispering secret wishes.
If I drive with my eyes closed,
I hear the far-off tinkling of two people
toasting with iced sarsaparilla,
the house where we are going,
where two people, once dead, are alive.

Acknowledgments

Grateful acknowledgment is made to the following journals in which some of the poems in this collection first appeared.

Asimov's Science Fiction: "All Saints Day"
Blueline: "Bark Eater," "My Beloved Is Like an Otter Again,"
Buddhist Poetry Review: "To the Bobcat That Sprang in Front
    of Our Car"
Calyx: "To Haplogroup K after DNA Testing"
Chiron Review: "To the Feral Pigs of Clinton County"
Cimarron Review: "Blueberry Crumble at the Noon-Time Diner"
Citron Review: "Valley of Dry Bones"
Cloudbank: "Shamata"
Connecticut River Review: "Cow Psalm"
Fugue: "My Sweet Little Pigeons"
Gone Lawn: "Eating Sadness"
Hamilton Stone Review: "Ezekiel," "If a Black Bea Approaches,"
    "Tick," "Why I Will Not Sell the Undeveloped Parcel"
Hotel Amerika: "To Be a Wintering Snake," "Transient Pleasures
    of the Animal Realm"
Massachusetts Review: "Monkey Spinning a Prayer Wheel"
New Ohio Review: "Black-Eyed Susan," "Life as Lucy," "Our
    Fathers," "Who Can Forget the Grannies"
PANK: "In the Biopsy Bardo"
Passager: "Woodchuck-a-Phobia"
Pine Hills Review: "Questions for the Arborist"
The Puritan: "Goats"
Slipstream: "Our Fathers"
The Southern Review: "Wild Pansy"
Strange Horizons: "Note to the Caretaker"
The Sun: "Love Song with Pigeons," "Not So Easy, Saving
    Sentient Beings"

Tenemos: "Obit"

Tiferet: "Yoho"

West Texas Literary Review: "God Is an Old Pear"

"Monkey Spinning a Prayer Wheel" was reprinted in *The Writers Studio at 30*, ed. Philip Schultz (Epiphany Editions, 2017).

"Wild Pansy" was reprinted at poets.org, the Academy of American Poetry website.

"Blueberry Crumble at the Noon-Time Diner," "Life as Lucy," "Love Song with Pigeons" (as "Love Poem"), "Monkey Spinning a Prayer Wheel," "My Sweet Little Pigeons," and "What I Found" appeared in *Nectar*, a limited edition chapbook (Encircle Publications, 2012), winner of The Aurorean Chapbook Prize.

"Black-Eyed Susan" received a 2017 Pushcart Special Mention.

"My Sweet Little Pigeons" received the 2008 Fugue Poetry Prize.

About the Author

Lisa Bellamy is author of the chapbook *Nectar*, which won The Aurorean chapbook prize in 2011. Her poems and prose have appeared in *TriQuarterly, Massachusetts Review, New Ohio Review, Hotel Amerika, The Southern Review, Cimarron Review*, and elsewhere. She has received a Pushcart Special Mention, the Fugue Poetry Prize, and honorable mention in *The Year's Best Fantasy and Horror*. She is a graduate of Princeton University and is on the faculty of The Writers Studio in NYC. She grew up in Wisconsin and now lives in Brooklyn and Upper Jay, NY.

www.lisabellamypoet.com